PSALMS

of

ALL MY DAYS

Books by Jennifer Grotz

Psalms of All My Days (translation)
The Needle
Cusp

PSALMS

of

ALL MY DAYS

Patrice de La Tour du Pin

Translated from the French
by
Jennifer Grotz

CARNEGIE MELLON UNIVERSITY PRESS
PITTSBURGH 2013

ACKNOWLEDGMENTS

Thank you to the editors of the following journals in which some of these poems (often in previous versions) first appeared:

American Poetry Review (Psalms 8, 9)
Antioch Review (Psalm 23)
Asheville Poetry Review (Psalms 7, 37)
Blackbird (Psalms 6, 18, 31, 32, 33)
Center (Psalm 26)
Circumference (Psalm 22)
Copper Nickel (Psalms 1, 5)
Lyric (Psalms 10, 12)
Mantis (Psalms 2, 17)
Narrative ("Laurence Sleeping," Psalms 21, 53, 56)
New England Review (Psalms 3, 4)
New South (Psalms 16, 29)
Ploughshares (Psalm 20)
Poetry International (Psalms 24, 36)
Tri-Quarterly ("September's Children")

Psalms 6, 25, 41, and 52 also appear in *Poems of Devotion: An Anthology of Recent Poets,* edited by Luke Hankins, Wipf and Stock Publishers, 2012.

Design by Sara-Anne Lee

Library of Congress Control Number 2012950943
ISBN 978-0-88748-572-5
Copyright © Jennifer Grotz
Printed and bound in the United States of America

10 9 8 7 6 5 4 3 2 1

Thank you to Catherine Savage Brosman, who first introduced me to the poems of Patrice de La Tour du Pin, and to Dorothy Z. Baker, whose help in the art of translation and encouragement of various kinds inspired me to undertake this project. Thank you also to Rosanna Warren whose gracious critiques improved a number of these translations substantially.

Thank you also to the American Literary Translators Association for a grant that aided in the completion of this book as well as to the Monastère de Saorge for residencies in which many of these translations were undertaken and revised.

MATIÈRES

CONTENTS

AN INTRODUCTION TO THE PSALMS OF PATRICE DE LA TOUR DU PIN

When I recently went back to read La Tour du Pin's own foreword to his final book, *Psalms of All My Days*, I was surprised to find something I'd somehow overlooked all the times before: he himself had had the same doubt about his endeavors that I did. "My first reaction at seeing them reassembled here is a certain uneasiness," La Tour du Pin writes of these collected psalms.

> It is quite dangerous to speak so much about God, to repeat continually his Name! One exposes oneself so easily to the risk of irritating, annoying, or provoking reflections primarily in terms of psychology or literary history whereas for the author, these terms hardly count by themselves and what he wanted was precisely to absorb them into an even more complete synthesis!

It's perhaps a treacherous admission for a translator to make, that she agrees with the poet's own reservations, but it is nonetheless salient to any frank introduction to this unusual poet. Like La Tour du Pin's own shifts in temper (the literal translation of his final book is more like *Psalms of All My Times*, though the French word for "time" is the same as "weather"), I found my opinions of the poet vacillating wildly during the course of this project, from utter admiration at a beautiful line or observation to cringing embarrassment at a moment I found naïve or clichéd to bewildered recognition at times, like what one might register with a relative or someone known a long time, that he was even stranger—but also more wonderful—than I'd originally thought.

He himself seems constantly to acknowledge the oddity of his own enterprise. And what was this enterprise? He named it and referred to it in different ways in his psalms, sometimes as his "dream to write the great prayer for mankind" to the assembling of an "interior liturgy," but most of the time, he described the desire to create his own world. When, in Psalm 18, he laments:

> Who would believe in my caverns, in my trees?

who will take my stones for real?

the reader registers that La Tour du Pin's self-doubt is almost, at times, actual embarrassment by his own creations. It's the odd anxiety of someone suddenly conscious of having created something for personal pleasure who then showed it to the world and now, unable to protect or defend the work, must sheepishly consider how it fares to an objective reader. It's a feeling any young poet knows. But the experience is confounded further by the fact that most of these psalms aren't addressed to the reader but directly to God. La Tour du Pin writes in Psalm 35:

> My most profound desire: to speak of you;
> my shame: to compromise you!
> So I will speak only to you.

This puts the reader in a curious place—one where she is invited to eavesdrop—and it is a vulnerable position for everyone involved. But perhaps this is not so uncommon for poetry. La Tour du Pin's poems illustrate convincingly J. S. Mill's famous assertion that "Eloquence is heard. Poetry is what's overheard." There's a recurring desire in the poems to remain humble and to avoid any sort of self-aggrandizing showiness:

> If you are possessed by the demon of speech,
> if you cannot resist him,
>
> strive to remain simple.
> A higher register will furnish you nothing

he writes in Psalm 14. Most commonly, as in the Biblical psalms, La Tour du Pin's figurative language resorts back to the natural world. He frequently refers to the act of writing as a kind of gardening; even more humbly, he sometimes likens it to being a seed or plant buried in God's ground, in need of sunlight's inspiration to grow.

> I make my poems the way an ash tree makes leaves—
> not light, that's not for an ash tree to do.
>
> Before you take me back entirely, Lord, I ask you kindly:
> dapple light upon my leaves. (Psalm 24)

What exactly did La Tour du Pin undertake in his poetry? Like other writers who combined religious longing with tremendous poetic ambition (we might think here perhaps of Dante, Milton, or Blake), he strove to erect a monumental architecture that combined his dual poetic and religious callings. He met unusual early success with his first publication at the age of twenty in the *Nouvelle Revue Française* of "September's Children," dedicated to the poet Jules Supervielle. He published his first book of poetry, *The Quest for Joy*, two years later, a collection of predominantly religious lyrics in various forms and rhyme schemes. The next thirty years or so would be devoted to creating what La Tour du Pin called his *Sum of Poetry*, a fifteen hundred-paged multi-genre work in which he incorporated all of his poems into a super-structure organized into three different volumes, each dedicated to the investigation of a certain "jeu" ("game" or "play"): *The Play of Man Before Himself*, *The Play of Man Before Others*, and *The Play of Man Before God*. Amid prose tracts, dramatic monologues, imagined landscapes and characters, epistolary passages, and poems of various kinds, La Tour du Pin interspersed his psalms.

Perhaps all of this would seem even more bizarre if La Tour du Pin had lived his life as a high-powered lawyer in Paris, say, or even as a professor at the Sorbonne. But in fact, after his formal education (he did actually study to be a lawyer at Paris's prestigious École de Sciences Politiques) and service in World War II (where he was taken prisoner and held in Germany until his repatriation in 1942—and even, through misinformation, was mistakenly reported in the French newspapers as having died), La Tour du Pin spent the remainder of his life exactly in pursuit of what he called "the reclusive life of poetry." Born into an old aristocratic family, he spent virtually all of his life in the family's chateau in the tiny village of Le Bignon-Mirabeau, about an hour south of Paris. This region of France, known as the Gâtinais, is the landscape of essentially all of La Tour du Pin's poetry, with its beautiful forests and marshlands as well as a variety of wildfowl to which La Tour du Pin once confessed an "almost physical attraction."

In his final years, La Tour du Pin's lifelong quests culminated in a professional success—the invitation of the Catholic Church, after Vatican II, to help compose the French liturgy—and a more personal one, that is, the publication of his final volume, *Psalms of All My Days*, in 1974, the year before he died. "I always reserved for myself the right," he observes in the foreword,

> to remake the sole book that I had dreamed of writing over the course of my entire life. Now that the hour has come and I am working on it, might I take advantage of an introduction to these remade psalms to explain to myself, not about this right, but rather on the significance of such a return? It seems to me to arise from some compulsion more secret and more vital than the simple motive of improving an insufficient fruit or of clarifying an overly obscure collection. I often hear it said that it is dangerous to return at the age of sixty to the texts of one's adolescence, that an author is not necessarily a good judge of his own work, and that if there is no new creative sap, silence and detachment are the best attitudes: all of that is quite reasonable. But already the simple fact of my having launched on such an unreasonable enterprise long ago seems to me to cover the going . . . and now the return.

For the most part, La Tour du Pin is in fact an excellent judge of his own work, and the exclusion of certain poems as well as the preserving, cutting and pruning he does to those he includes in this final work is almost exclusively in service of the individual poems. But the reader will note that my own selections for translation reside heavily in the first half of the book (arranged chronologically), for the final section in particular loses its productive poetic doubt and reads more liturgically. "Liturgy," as E. M. Cioran once noted in the case of religious mystics, "is an enemy of style." However, like the Biblical Psalms, La Tour du Pin's final collection of these lyrics creates a history or path of sorts of the spiritual life. Translating these, I have thought countless times of Dietrich Bonhoeffer's reminder that the *entire* book of the Psalms, with its complaints as well as its thanksgivings, was the richest model we were given to pray.

* * *

It would be hard to overestimate the importance of the book of *Psalms* on Western literature. In France, the Biblical Psalms were first translated from Latin into the vernacular in the early sixteenth century, an act of great bravery at the time, in fact, for it was forbidden by the Sorbonne that Psalms be translated because such an endeavor was synonymous with an act of Protestantism. Clément Marot, by the time of his death in 1544, translated fifty psalms from the Latin version of the Psalter made by Saint Jerome. In addition to vernacular translations, subsequent writers in the late sixteenth and early seventeenth century wrote paraphrases of the psalms (a similar process unfolded in England as well). Paraphrases led to imitations, including the odd work of Sylvain Maréchal, a declared atheist, who claimed to have found and translated some "Psalms Lost in the Flood" in 1784.

In the twentieth century, Paul Claudel completed his own book of translations of the Psalms. In his own poetry, he adopted the early Psalms' signature form of the "verset," that sonorous long-line that hovers between poetry and prose but remains linked to the unit of the breath, a line we think of as "Biblical" (and perhaps Whitmanic). La Tour du Pin's psalms do not attempt to translate or paraphrase the Biblical Psalms. Nor, for his significant attention to their numbering and sequencing, do they employ any kind of parsible numerology. Nevertheless, he adopts, like Claudel, many of the Psalms's formal features that were slowly disappearing after centuries of translation. In addition to the verset, we normally associate the notion of parallelism with the psalms. C. S. Lewis, in his wonderful handbook, *Reflections on the Psalms*, observes that

> [i]t is (according to one's point of view) either a wonderful piece of luck or a wise provision of God's, that poetry which was to be turned into all languages should have as its chief formal characteristic one that does not disappear (as mere metre does) in translation.

Lewis goes on to point out how often Jesus in the Bible speaks using parallelism, as in "Ask, and it shall be given you; seek, and ye shall find; knock and it shall be opened unto you." Touchingly, he concludes, "Humanly speaking, He would have learned this style, if from no one else . . . from His Mother." A similar structural adaption frequently employed by La Tour du Pin is what is often called the psalm's "envelope" structure, that is the tendency to end a psalm with a return to the imagery or assertion used at its beginning.

* * *

In some ways, I think of what La Tour du Pin called his "théopoésie" or "theo-poetry" more as a kind of meta-poetry, one that concerns itself with a constant combing through the self's desires and perceptions so as to cleanse and to clarify them. Although I often find most moving the psalms that culminate in a moment of fear or bewilderment, there is a real sense that La Tour du Pin gauged his own poetic success at being able to speak as honestly as possible in the poem and for it nevertheless by grace or inspiration to veer towards gratitude and thanksgiving at the end.

Every translator knows all too well the Italian saying, "*Traductore, tradditore*" (To translate [is] to betray). If I have betrayed La Tour du Pin, it is perhaps in my choice not to preserve the psalms in their original contexts. The collection opens with three brief lyrics, ones for which La Tour du Pin received early acclaim, but the remainder of the poems included are all taken from La Tour du Pin's final selection and revision of his own psalms. Taking more of a poet's approach than a scholar's, I have tried instead to assemble the poems that I felt were the strongest as poems and also ones I felt most able to render successfully into English. Nonetheless, such a choice betrays my judgment that La Tour du Pin's literary architecture was ultimately less successful than his individual lyrics. And so I take small comfort, as I mentioned at the beginning of this introduction, that La Tour du Pin, who likewise culled these psalms originally, in his words, "drowned in long prose texts or sequences in poems," worried nonetheless as I have.

La Tour du Pin is interesting in part exactly for the way he doesn't seem to fit into his own century (but perhaps we could say the same about other reclusive visionaries such as William Blake, Emily Dickinson, perhaps even Rilke). It's not hard to understand why he has been left out of the usual narrative of avant-garde poetry in early twentieth-century France. He is still relatively unknown and more or less out of fashion in current French letters, although a 2005 colloquium at the Collège de France, in addition to the even more recent appearance of critical essays and monographs, point towards a renewed interest in the poet's work. Perhaps the greatest living French poet, Yves Bonnefoy, attended the 2005 colloquium and named La Tour du Pin as "a poet who counts for me." Whether or not the English reader will come to count La Tour du Pin as an essential poet remains to be seen, but he is nevertheless a moving and revelatory example of a poet pursuing "his fragile quest for God in the middle of the twentieth century" and a reminder that poetry can still be made anywhere, out of anything, and by anyone devoted to developing the craft and talent to sing.

ENFANTS DE SEPTEMBRE

à Jules Supervielle

Les bois étaient tout recouverts de brumes basses,
Déserts, gonflés de pluie et silencieux;
Longtemps avait soufflé ce vent du Nord où passent
Les Enfants Sauvages, fuyant vers d'autres cieux,
Par grands voiliers, le soir, et très haut dans l'espace.

J'avais senti siffler leurs ailes dans la nuit,
Lorsqu'ils avaient baissé pour chercher les ravines
Où tout le jour, peut-être, ils resteront enfouis;
Et cet appel inconsolé de sauvagine
Triste, sur les marais que les oiseaux ont fuis.

Après avoir surpris le dégel de ma chambre,
A l'aube, je gagnai la lisière des bois;
Par une bonne lune de brouillard et d'ambre,
Je relevai la trace, incertaine parfois,
Sur le bord d'un layon, d'un enfant de Septembre.

Les pas étaient légers et tendres, mais brouillés,
Ils se croisaient d'abord au milieu des ornières
Où dans l'ombre, tranquille, il avait essayé
De boire, pour reprendre ses jeux solitaires
Très tard, après le long crépuscule mouillé.

Et puis, ils se perdaient plus loin parmi les hêtres
Où son pied ne marquait qu'à peine sur le sol;
Je me suis dit: il va s'en retourner peut-être
A l'aube, pour chercher ses compagnons de vol,
En tremblant de la peur qu'ils aient pu disparaître.

SEPTEMBER'S CHILDREN

to Jules Supervielle

The woods were thick with low mist,
Silent, deserted, swollen with rain;
Long had blown the North wind carrying
The Untamed Children fleeing in the dark
Among the migratory birds high above.

I heard the whirring of wings in the night
From when they flew low to search the ravines
Where by day, perhaps, they might hide;
I heard the wildfowl's inconsolable cry
On the marsh the birds had fled.

After cold had filled my room and woke me,
I went at dawn to the wood's edge;
Under a clouded moon, an amber moonlight,
I followed the tracks, sometimes uncertain,
Along the edge of a trail, of a child of September.

Light and gentle were his footsteps, but also confused,
First they cut across the middle of the path
To where in peaceful dark he had tried
To drink before his solitary amusements began
Long after twilight's wet lingering.

And then he'd gotten lost further off in the beeches
Where his feet had only barely touched the ground;
I told myself: perhaps at dawn he will return here
To look for his flying companions, trembling
From fear that they had disappeared.

Il va certainement venir dans ces parages
A la demi-clarté qui monte à l'orient,
Avec les grandes bandes d'oiseaux de passage,
Et les cerfs inquiets qui cherchent dans le vent
L'heure d'abandonner le calme des gagnages.

Le jour glacial s'était levé sur les marais;
Je restais accroupi dans l'attente illusoire,
Regardant défiler la faune qui rentrait
Dans l'ombre, les chevreuils peureux qui venaient boire
Et les corbeaux criards aux cimes des forêts.

Et je me dis: je suis un enfant de Septembre,
Moi-même, par le cœur, la fièvre et l'esprit,
Et la brûlante volupté de tous mes membres,
Et le désir que j'ai de courir dans la nuit
Sauvage, ayant quitté l'étouffement des chambres.

Il va certainement me traiter comme un frère,
Peut-être me donner un nom parmi les siens;
Mes yeux le combleraient d'amicales lumières
S'il ne prenait pas peur, en me voyant soudain
Les bras ouverts, courir vers lui dans la clairière.

Farouche, il s'enfuira comme un oiseaux blessé,
Je le suivrai jusqu'à ce qu'il demande grâce,
Jusqu'à ce qu'il s'arrête en plein ciel, épuisé,
Traqué jusqu'à la mort, vaincu, les ailes basses,
Et les yeux résignés à mourir, abaissés.

Surely he will come back to this very spot
In the half-light that rises in the east,
Where the migratory birds flock
And the stags nervously study the wind
For the signal to abandon the field's calm.

The frigid day rose across the marsh;
I stayed crouched in illusive waiting,
Watching the fawn step back into shadow,
The fearful deer that came to drink
And the crows squawking from the treetops.

And I told myself: I am a child of September,
Me too, in my heart, my fever, my spirit,
In the burning thrill in each of my limbs
And the desire I have to run wild in the night,
Leaving behind the suffocation of rooms.

He will surely treat me like a brother,
Perhaps he'll give me a name among the others;
He'll see my eyes filled with friendship
If he does not turn fearful when I
Rush toward him in the clearing with open arms.

Timid, he might flee like a wounded bird,
I will follow him until he asks for mercy,
Until he stops in the open air, exhausted,
Hunted to the moment of his defeat, wings fallen
And with eyes lowered in resignation to death.

Alors, je le prendrai dans mes bras, endormi,
Je le caresserai sur la pente des ailes,
Et je ramènerai son petit corps, parmi
Les roseaux, rêvant à des choses irréelles,
Réchauffé tout le temps par mon sourire ami . . .

Mais les bois étaient recouverts de brumes basses
Et le vent commençait à remonter au Nord,
Abandonnant tous ceux dont les ailes sont lasses,
Tous ceux qui sont perdus et tous ceux qui sont morts,
Qui vont par d'autres voies en de mêmes espaces!

Et je me suis dit: Ce n'est pas dans ces pauvres landes
Que les enfants de Septembre vont s'arrêter;
Un seul qui se serait écarté de sa bande
Aurait-il, en un soir, compris l'atrocité
De ces marais déserts et privés de légende?

That's when I'll take him sleeping in my arms,
I will caress the downward slope of his wings,
And I will carry his small body among the reeds
While he is lost in unreal dreams
Kindled meanwhile by my friendly smile . . .

But the woods were thick with low mist
And the wind began to rise to the North,
Abandoning all whose wings are weary,
All who are lost and all who are dying,
Those who take paths headed in other directions!

And I told myself: Not here, in these poor heaths
Will September's children come to rest;
Should one of them—separated from the others—
Could he, in a night, comprehend the horror
Of this marsh deserted and deprived of legend?

LÉGENDE

Va dire à ma chère Ile, là-bas, tout là-bas,
Près de cet obscur marais de Foulc, dans la lande,
Que je viendrai vers elle ce soir, qu'elle attende,
Qu'au lever de la lune elle entendra mon pas.

Tu la trouveras baignant ses pieds sous les rouches,
Les cheveux dénoués, les yeux clos à demi,
Et naïve, tenant une main sur la bouche,
Pour ne pas réveiller les oiseaux endormis.

Car les marais sont tout embués de légende,
Comme le ciel que l'on découvre dans ses yeux,
Quand ils boivent la bonne lune sur la lande
Ou les vents tristes qui dévalent des Hauts-Lieux.

Dis-lui que j'ai passé des aubes merveilleuses
A guetter les oiseaux qui revenaient du nord,
Si près d'elle, étendue à mes pieds et frileuse
Comme une petite sauvagine qui dort.

Dis-lui que nous voici vers la fin de septembre,
Que les hivers sont durs dans ces pays perdus,
Que devant la croisée ouverte de ma chambre,
De grands fouillis de fleurs sont toujours répandus.

Annonce-moi comme un prophète, comme un prince,
Comme le fils d'un roi d'au-delà de la mer;
Dis-lui que les parfums inondent mes provinces
Et que les Hauts-Pays ne souffrent pas l'hiver.

LEGEND

Go tell my dear Isle, there, way out there,
Close to that dim Foulc marsh on the moor,
That I will come to her tonight, she should wait for me,
That at moonrise she will hear my step.

You'll find her bathing her feet in the water,
Hair undone, eyes half closed
And holding a naïve hand to her mouth
Not to wake the sleeping birds.

For the marsh is everywhere imbued with legend,
Just like the sky one can find in her eyes
When they are drinking up the moon on the moor
Or the sad winds that rush down from the Highlands.

Tell her that I've spent marvelous dawns
Watching for birds that return from the north
So close to her, stretched out at my feet and shivering
Like a small wildfowl asleep.

Tell her that here we are at the end of September,
That the winters are hard in this land forlorn,
That outside my room's open window
Are always scattered great tangles of flowers.

Announce me like a prophet, like a prince,
Like the son of a king from across the sea;
Tell her that my provinces overflow with perfumes
And that the Highlands never suffer winter.

Dis-lui que les balcons ici seront fleuris,
Qu'elle se baignera dans les étangs sans fièvre,
Mais que je voudrais voir dans ses yeux assombris
Le sauvage secret qui se meurt sur ses lèvres,

L'énigme d'un regard de pure transparence
Et qui brille parfois du fascinant éclair
Des grands initiés aux jeux de connaissance
Et des couleurs du large, sous les cieux déserts . . .

Tell her the balconies here are covered in flowers,
That she can bathe in the ponds without catching fever,
But that I would like to find in her somber eyes
The wild secret that dies on her lips,

The enigma of a purely transparent regard
That flashes sometimes with the fascination
Of those initiated in games of knowledge
And an expanse of color under deserted skies . . .

LAURENCE ENDORMIE

Cette odeur sur les pieds, de narcisse et de menthe
Parce qu'ils ont foulé dans leur course légère
Fraîches écloses, les fleurs des nuits printanières
Remplira tout mon cœur de ses vagues dormantes;

Et peut-être très loin sur ces jambes polies,
Tremblant de la caresse encor de l'herbe haute,
Ce parfum végétal qui monte, lorsque j'ôte
Tes bas éclaboussés de rosée ou de pluie;

Jusqu'à cette rancœur du ventre pâle et lisse
Où l'ambre et la sueur divinement se mêlent
Aux pétales séchés au milieu des dentelles
Quand sur les pentes d'ombre inerte mes mains glissent,

Laurence... jusqu'aux flux brûlants de ta poitrine,
Gonflée et toute crépitante de lumière
Hors de la fauve floraison des primevères
Où s'épuisent en vain ma bouche et mes narines,

Jusqu'à la senteur lourde de ta chevelure,
Éparse sur le sol comme une étoile blonde,
Où tu as répandu tous les parfums du monde
Pour assouvir enfin la soif qui me torture!

LAURENCE SLEEPING

This scent of narcissus and mint rising up
From feet on their light way that have
Crushed a spring night's fresh blooms
Swells my heart's dormant waves;

And such organic perfume rises
All the way up these polished legs
Still trembling from the caress of tall grasses
While I remove your stockings splashed with rain or dew;

Up to the sharp scent at the stomach, smooth and pale,
Where sweat and amber divinely combine
With dried petals on a bed of lace while
Over slopes of motionless shadow glide my hands,

Laurence . . . up to the burning surge of
Your chest, inflated and rippled with light
Beyond the musky bloom of primrose, where
My mouth and nostrils exhaust themselves in vain,

Up to the heavy scent of your hair
Spread like a blond star across the ground
Where you have spilled the whole world's perfumes
To assuage at last this thirst that consumes!

PSAUME 1

Est-il mort en vénérateur de lui-même,
la tête entre les jambes et les mains jointes?

Au dernier spasme, était-il en révolte
d'être défait si absurdement?

Alors qu'il n'avait pas fait éclore toute la lumière qu'il couvait,
pas atteint toute sa taille.

Le voici muet, Seigneur, ses amis le remplacent,
tu permets que cela soit ainsi.

C'est en son nom que nous pouvons te dire:
oui, j'ai trop aimé la grandeur.

Oui, j'ai jeté ma vie dans la passion d'écrire,
j'ai savouré le dégoût du vulgaire.

Mais si je fus un riche d'esprit couché sur un trésor,
jamais je ne l'ai vraiment tenu pour le mien.

Écoute le témoignage de ses amis, Seigneur,
oublie ce que nous oublions.

Et retiens seulement de ton serviteur
qu'il a voulu redresser le jeu de l'homme vers toi.

PSALM 1

With his head between his legs and hands joined,
was he bowing to himself when he died?

And his final spasm, was it in protest
of such an absurd defeat?

For the flame that bloomed inside him
never flared to its great height.

His friends stand in for him, Lord, now that he is silent,
you allow it to be like this.

It's in his name that we can speak to you:
yes, I loved greatness too much.

I threw myself into the passion of writing;
I savored the disgust of the vulgar.

But if I felt like a rich man sleeping on his treasure,
I never truly took it for my own.

Listen to his friends' accounts, Lord,
overlook what we have overlooked

And remember only that your servant
wanted humanity's way set right for you.

PSAUME 2

Doit-on nommer orgueil cette ambition de faire un monde,
volupté spirituelle, son façonnement?

Ô ils sont brefs, les instants de jouissance!
il faut sans cesse le brasser, le souffler.

Sans cesse y apporter des ressources nouvelles,
y faire confluer d'autres sangs que le mien.

Avais-je en moi de la semence de prophète,
et le germe des saints que j'ai cherché à susciter?

J'ai fait des enfants d'inquiétude pour le plaisir,
de hautes intelligences par jalousie.

Et j'ai aimé ce peuple passionné,
oui, je l'avoue, je me suis aimé en poésie.

Était-ce vraiment m'aimer moi-même?
rien ne m'attire à moi lorsque je m'en dévêts.

Toi seul connais le jeu qui me force à sa cause,
toi seul peux m'en sauver—ou le sauver.

PSALM 2

Must we call it pride, this ambition to make a world,
the spiritual delight in its shaping?

O they are brief, such moments of joy!
I must constantly stir, blow upon it,

Constantly carry it to new springs,
mingle it with blood other than my own.

Did I have a prophet's seed in me, or
did I inherit from the saints I'd searched to rouse?

I made the restless children for the pleasure of it,
the high intellects from jealousy.

And I loved this impassioned people,
yes, I admit it, I loved myself in poetry.

Was it really just loving myself?
nothing attracts me to myself when I undress.

You alone understand this play that compels me to its end,
you alone can save me from it—or save it.

PSAUME 3

Et voici que des sens négligés me dévorent,
moi qui ne comptais rien engendrer de ma chair.

Je m'étais promis de vivre seul pour mon livre:
à moi seul, j'avais fait ce vœu, pas à toi!

Je m'étais retranché dans une île,
mes sens et mon esprit tendus vers un même fruit.

La loi des mâles me résiste,
elle exige de les séparer.

Il y a des nuits où il viendrait seulement un oiseau dans mon île
que je prendrais dans mon lit.

Les médecins disent que c'est exécrable,
les conseilleurs spirituels hochent la tête.

Faut-il que je déchire ma promesse?
je ne t'ai pas prié de la retenir.

Il y avait là pourtant un beau rêve,
le rêve d'un autre engendrement de la vie.

PSALM 3

And now my neglected senses devour me,
I who counted on begetting nothing from my flesh.

I had promised myself to live alone for my book:
to myself alone I made this vow, not to you!

I withdrew to an island so that
my body and spirit could labor toward the same fruit,

away from the law of males
which demands the two remain separate.

There were nights only a bird would come to my island
that I would take into my bed.

The doctors say this is detestable,
the spiritual counselors lower their heads.

Do I have to break my promise?
I never prayed to you to keep it.

Yet it was a beautiful dream out there,
the dream of another kind of creation.

PSAUME 4

Parce que je chante parfois les anges,
on croit que j'aspire à leur pureté.

Ils me font rire, mes interprètes,
ceux qui pensent que j'ai honte de ma chair!

Mais dois-je dormir seul à perte de vie,
demeurer seul avec ma vie?

Mon désir remonte à mes dents,
je suis pris par la rage des fauves.

Ils se tournent contre ma vie et la mordent,
mes déserts se peuplent d'eux en un instant.

Je ne me croyais pas une terre pour leur espèce,
le besoin de ma chair en suscite partout.

J'avais mal exploré mes solitudes,
je croyais qu'elles n'en appelaient qu'à toi.

Vers toi à travers ta création peut-être,
vers tes anges qui doivent y passer.

Elles ne demandent que la tendresse,
la fraîcheur d'un sourire féminin.

Non, ce n'est pas ma chair que je redoute,
mais de n'avoir pas assez d'amour à donner.

PSALM 4

Because I sing sometimes of angels,
some believe I aspire to their purity.

They make me laugh, my critics,
those who think I'm ashamed of my flesh!

Yet must I sleep alone for the rest of my life,
remain all alone with this life?

Desire rises up to my teeth.
Wild beasts overtake me,

Beasts that turn against me and attack with fangs,
that in an instant populate the desert of my soul.

I didn't think my body was a home for their kind,
but incessant desire resuscitates them.

I had barely explored my solitudes,
I believed the beasts were only calling out to you.

To you and your creations, perhaps,
to your angels who are always passing through.

They are only asking for tenderness,
the freshness of a woman's smile.

No, it's not my flesh I question
but of not having enough love to give.

PSAUME 5

Il a volé un peu de mon âme à ses seigneurs,
il s'y est reposé quelques instants.

Au matin il n'était plus qu'un souvenir,
et les seigneurs ont dit: Soyons tranquilles, il est passé.

Ils ont repris possession de leurs terres,
clamant: Que nous importe? c'est déjà du passé.

Pourtant ils se sont inquiétés de ses traces,
de son rappel comme à demeure en ma mémoire.

Un moment de tendresse qu'il a eu avec moi,
et j'ai été creusé pour la vie.

Mes seigneurs se sont dit: Il monte, il remonte,
le voici qui fait face au présent ça et là.

Un jour, il ne sera plus le vivant caché dans la mémoire,
un jour il paraîtra.

Du fond des sources, de derrière les collines,
de toutes les pentes vers le désert et vers la mer.

Il devance la mort, il remonte certainement avant la mort,
et quand la mort tombera, il surgira à côté d'elle.

PSALM 5

He stole a bit of my soul from its usual lords;
for a few moments he rested there.

By morning it was just a memory,
and my lords said: Let's be calm, it's over now.

They took possession of their grounds again,
proclaiming: What does it matter to us? It's already in the past.

Yet they worried over the traces of him
still lodged in my memory.

One moment of tenderness he had with me,
and I was hollowed for life.

My lords told each other: he'll rise up, he'll rise back up,
here or there, he's going to resurface.

One day, he will no longer be living memory hiding in me,
one day he will appear.

From the spring's source, from behind the hills,
from every slope leading to desert or sea.

He comes before death, he certainly rises back up before death,
and when death falls, he will surge by its side.

PSAUME 6

Voici que j'ai rêvé d'écrire la grande prière
de l'Homme de ce temps . . .

La grandeur me harcèle sans cesse:
jamais je n'aurais droit à cette voix.

J'en prends d'autres bien sûr dans le choeur de mon âme,
celles qui me viennent par le sang ou l'amitié.

Des cris de hasard et des appels à une même grâce,
même des échos avec qui j'ai peine à communier.

C'est ainsi que je fais une liturgie intérieure,
que je trouve un grand nombre en demeurant en moi.

Si mon beau rêve est dérisoire, Seigneur,
souffle sur lui, car il me tient.

Il me dirige dans mes recherches. . .
ah! peut-il exister une grâce de poésie?

J'ai bien cette espérance qui m'aimante,
plus tenace parfois que mes démons.

Mais en elle s'infiltre aussi la soif de l'Homme,
ma plus intime liturgie voudrait être la plus intime de chacun.

On doit pouvoir trouver le cri des autres,
rien qu'à creuser en soi vers un appel commun.

PSALM 6

Then I came to dream of writing
the great prayer of our time . . .

This ambition plagues me constantly:
I could never have the right to such a voice.

I draw of course from the choir of voices in my soul,
voices that come to me through blood or friendship,

Chance cries and calls for a same grace,
even echoes of those I've barely encountered.

I assemble an interior liturgy in this way,
by finding the great number who reside in me.

If my dream is laughable, Lord,
extinguish it, for it consumes me.

It guides me in what I seek:
could poetry be a kind of grace?

I hold on to this lovely hope
more tenacious at times than my demons.

But human thirst infiltrates it as well:
my most intimate liturgy would like to be each one's most intimate.

One must be able to hear the cry of others, to do nothing but
empty the self for the sake of a common call.

Ton cri d'amour et ta plainte par les autres:
alors je ne ris plus: tu me tiens.

Your love cry and your lament in the voice of others:
so I stop laughing: you hold me.

PSAUME 7

Le poète amoureux du Christ a dit à ceux qui l'écoutaient:
je ne suis pas le poète christique.

Ceux qui m'appellent de ce nom m'ignorent:
que ne dirais-je, si j'étais une telle terre d'élection?

Je n'ai pas d'autre titre que de champ de sa terre,
il est déjà lourd à porter.

Et je dois cultiver ce champ dans mon poème,
dans mon souffle où rien ne m'est dicté.

Si je t'exalte, Seigneur, c'est en mots périssables,
ils retombent sur moi comme des feuilles d'hiver.

Et voilà qu'une nouvelle saison commence,
mes racines vont sucer à leur décomposition.

Mes jeunes feuilles sont aussi éphémères,
je ne suis pas capable d'éternelles floraisons.

Alors pourquoi m'assomme-t-on d'un titre si sublime?
vais-je me parer de lui parce que je crie vers toi?

J'arroserai mon champ avec l'eau que tu dis,
j'exposerai mes plantes à la lumière que tu dis.

Ton jardinier s'affaire, creuse la terre pour le ciel:
Par grâce, avant toute chose, tu lui as pris sa mort.

PSALM 7

The poet in love with Christ said to those who would listen:
I am not "the Christ poet."

Those who call me by that name don't know about me:
if I were such chosen ground, wouldn't I say so?

I have no title other than field on his earth—
that alone is hard to carry.

And in my poem I must cultivate this field,
with my own breath, where nothing is dictated to me.

If I exalt you, Lord, it's with words that perish,
that fall back down on me like leaves in winter.

And this is how a new season begins,
my roots drink up their decomposition.

My new leaves are just as ephemeral—
I'm not capable of eternal blooms.

So why do they injure me with a title so sublime?
am I to assume his name because I cry out to you?

I will drench my field with the water you speak,
I will sun my plants with the light you speak.

Your gardener keeps busy, he ploughs the ground for the sky:
By grace, before all else, you took his death away from him.

PSAUME 8

Je voudrais arriver à la douceur des âmes
qui n'ont pas eu besoin d'arriver jusque-là.

Parce qu'elles ont reçu cette grâce à leur naissance
et qu'elles l'ont exploitée avec fidélité.

Parce qu'elles ont aimé pacifier, rendre grâce,
et souffler sur le jet de vie des autres sans le briser.

J'en suis encore à justifier mes répugnances,
à endurcir ma dureté.

J'élève mon orgueil pour ses hautes blessures:
il se redresse, même touché à mort.

Il s'écarte de ceux qui ne peuvent me suivre,
il écarte tous ceux qui veulent m'accompagner.

Je ne suis pourtant pas la chair de mon orgueil
et ta grâce me prie toujours de l'incarner.

Alors toute ma force se retourne en faiblesse,
tu me découvres qu'il faut toujours te chercher.

PSALM 8

I would like to attain the gentleness of souls
who never have to try to be gentle.

Because they received such grace at birth
and then employed it faithfully.

Because they loved to bring peace, to give grace,
to blow softly upon, without breaking, the streaming jet of other lives.

I am still someone who tries to justify my loathing,
determined to harden myself.

I lift up my wounded pride:
even on the verge of death, it stands tall.

It backs away from those who cannot follow me,
it pushes away all who want to accompany me.

I am not, however, my pride made flesh
and your grace still asks for me to incarnate it.

So all my power comes back as weakness,
and you show me that I must always seek you.

PSAUME 9

J'ai donné de mon temps pour sauver une bête . . .
tout est d'un même corps de création.

Quelle folie d'espérer en dire davantage,
le traduire avec mon seul monde en formation!

J'ai beau me retourner sur ma candeur d'enfance,
m'acharner à la déterrer du passé.

Elle ne me convient plus, je n'aurai plus de joies si pures . . .
dans tes réserves, tu en as.

De mon âme d'enfant, je te rapportais toute chose,
je t'aurais demandé de ranimer un oiseau mort.

Tu as laissé peser sur moi la loi de l'âge,
mais en m'offrant toujours ton secret pour éclore.

Refuge de poésie et refuge contre elle,
joie-mère de poésie et tristesse de ses fruits.

Joie-mère de beauté et de toutes amours,
tristesse-mère de beauté et tristesse-mère d'amour.

PSALM 9

I spent some of my time trying to save an animal . . .
everything comes from the same body of creation.

It's madness to say anything more about it, to hope
to explain it in terms of my own still-forming world.

However hard I try to return to the naivete of childhood,
try desperately to unearth it from the past,

It no longer fits me, I'll have no more of such pure joys . . .
in your reserves now, that's where you keep them.

With my child's mind, I used to bring you everything,
I'd ask you to bring a dead bird back to life.

You let the law of aging weigh upon me, but always
while offering me your secret of how to be born.

The refuge of poetry and refuge against it,
the joy-mother of poetry and the sorrow of its fruits.

The joy-mother of beauty and of all loves,
the sorrow-mother of beauty and the sorrow-mother of love.

PSAUME 10

Je ne suis plus le renard en chasse dans les prairies,
mais le faon qui trouve en elles sa pâture.

Parfois le goût du sang me remonte à la gorge,
comme aux princes de proie retirés dans leurs tours.

Ils se défendent de sortir pour de nouvelles conquêtes,
et portent le deuil des conquérants qu'ils ont été.

Ils remisent leurs trophées et leurs armes,
ils relâchent leurs faucons bien dressés.

Mais ils tiennent serrée leur passion d'aventure
sans plus chercher à prendre ou à tuer.

Ceux qui courent l'ivresse en dehors de leurs terres,
ne savent pas les sources qu'on goûte en la creusant.

Ils vont toujours plus loin par des vols de hasard:
moi, je pars des lointains pour trouver l'homme.

Et je n'ai pas besoin de boussole ou de rose des vents
pour aborder aux prairies en moi-même.

PSALM 10

I am no longer the fox hunting in the meadow
but the fawn who finds her pasture there.

Sometimes the taste of blood rises up again in my throat,
as it does to princes of prey withdrawn to their towers.

They refrain from seeking new conquests
and mourn the conquerors they once were.

They put away their trophies and their weapons,
they release their well-trained falcons.

But while no longer seeking to plunder or kill,
they keep close their passion for risk.

Those who chase drunkenness beyond their own lands
don't taste the springs one drinks from digging deep.

The winds of chance are always carrying them off—
but I depart for distant lands to search mankind

And find I have no need for map or compass
to reach those meadows in myself.

PSAUME 11

Quand ta lumière fait mal, c'est l'enfer,
c'est le feu qui calcine, et non celui qui prend en lui.

Ah! l'espérance de devenir particule de ta lumière,
tu l'as mêlée en moi au vieux feu de ma vie!

Est-ce elle qui me travaille pour décrire l'enfer
en ténèbre extérieure et réfractaire à toi?

Je bute à chaque image que j'ébauche,
j'efface la grande plaine charbonneuse qui ne prend pas.

Qu'ai-je à faire d'images inutiles?
je me fourvoie dans le métier que tu m'apprends.

Il me suffit de dire la jalousie des êtres
condamnés pour toujours à un stade inférieur.

Je me retrouve alors dans l'espérance de ta lumière,
je rentre en elle et je l'entends

Qui te supplie de baptiser tous les hommes
après leur mort, dans l'eau et dans le sang.

PSALM 11

When your light hurts, it's hell, it's fire
that incinerates, not consumes.

If only to become just a particle of your light!
Into my life's old flame you've mixed such a hope.

Is that what makes me describe this hell
in a darkness external and resistant to you?

I hesitate over each image I sketch,
I erase what doesn't work, the whole charcoal plain of it.

What am I to do with such useless images?
I lose my way in the craft you teach me.

For me it's enough to tell of the jealousy of beings
forever condemned to an inferior station.

Then I find myself again in the hope of your brightness,
I re-enter it and listen for

that which implores you to baptize every man
after their death in water and in blood.

PSAUME 12

Ils m'accusent d'être un migrateur
et de changer de lieu de pose sans arrêt.

Qu'y puis-je? le cœur de l'un est une lagune aride,
la profondeur de l'autre est bien trop ravagée.

Celui-ci peut montrer un jardin de délices,
celui-là n'exhale même pas un goût de terre dans la voix.

Je chevauche un moment avec l'homme d'aventure,
je plane quelques instants sur les plans d'eau de l'endormi.

Ils me reprochent une amitié de passage,
ils ne savent pas que je ramène chez moi mes amis.

Car je rentre en mon cœur, je suis une eau stagnante,
et ils viennent planer sur moi comme je planais.

Je chevauche en esprit avec mon compagnon de voyage,
j'offre un terrain nu à mon confident jardinier.

Je rappelle à mes prés qu'ils deviendront arides,
à mes vallées que tout finit par être ravagé.

Non, je ne me laisse pas apprivoiser par ceux que j'aime:
ma loi de migrateur, ils peuvent la détester.

Mais mon amitié ne se mesure pas au temps que je passe dans leurs âmes:
leur solitude, je me défends d'y pénétrer.

PSALM 12

They accuse me of being a wanderer
and of ceaselessly changing positions.

What can I do? The heart of one is a dry lagoon,
the mountain of another is completely leveled.

This one might display a garden of delights,
that one doesn't exude even a handful of earth in his voice.

I ride one moment with the man of adventure,
I glide a few moments on the smooth lake of the sleeper.

They reproach my passing friendships, not knowing
I bring my friends back home with me.

For when I come back to my heart, I am stagnant water,
and they come to linger by me as I lingered.

I ride in spirit with my travel companion,
I offer myself as bare ground for my friend to garden.

I remind my meadows that they will become arid
and tell my valleys that everything ends by being razed.

No, I won't let myself be tamed by those I love:
my wanderer's code, let them despise it.

My friendship isn't measured by the time I spend in their souls:
their loneliness—I won't allow myself to penetrate.

PSAUME 13

Il a remué, le cœur de mon cœur d'homme!
et voici que mon psaume s'élève comme une marée.

Il n'est pas né d'un simple penchant de mon cœur,
il monte de la vie qui se sécrète à travers lui.

Elle soulève mes sens et s'en habille,
elle se rue par ma gorge étroite vers mes lèvres.

A la surface, qu'en reste-t-il dans mon psaume?
les mots qu'elle a voulu charger n'en éclatent pas.

Ce n'est plus qu'un silence intraduisible par la parole:
mon silence vivant témoigne qu'elle meurt.

L'état de poésie n'est pas un coup de fièvre,
ni le ravissement stupéfait d'un moment.

On le surprend à ces signes éphémères,
mais il règne à demeure plus profond.

Quand il me gagne, c'est un nuage qui monte,
c'est le jet d'une vague vers le ciel.

Ils se heurtent à leur limite et ils retombent,
ils touchent à la folie de te demander raison.

Alors sur mon psaume à terre je me penche,
sur la trace du bond que j'ai voulu fixer.

PSALM 13

It stirred, the heart of my human heart!
so now my psalm rises like a tide.

It doesn't come from the heart's simple propensity,
it rises up out of life's secretions.

The tide stirs my senses and dresses itself in them,
it rushes through my throat straight to my lips.

And once at the surface, what of it remains in my psalm?
the words it meant to carry do not burst forth.

It's only a silence untranslatable by speech:
my living silence witnesses it die.

The state of poetry is not a fever blow,
nor a moment's astounded rapture.

One catches it in these ephemeral forms
but it rules a residence more profound.

When it overtakes me, it's a rising cloud,
it's a stream of waves gushing toward the sky.

They fling themselves to the limit and fall back down,
they reach toward the madness of asking you why.

So I lean over my psalm on the ground,
above where I'd wanted there to be a leap.

Il ne me reste plus que le silence des nuages,
le mutisme des eaux et des sens essoufflés.

Je retombe moi-même à la terre en attente,
devant toi, je ne peux pas désespérer.

Nothing remains for me but the silence of clouds,
the muteness of waters and the winded senses.

I fall back down upon the earth, expectant.
Before you, I cannot give up hope.

PSAUME 14

Quoi! vous prétendez dire votre tragédie intérieure!
vous oubliez que dire est une énigme aussi.

Le vide que vous souffrez ne rend qu'un seul murmure:
nul mot ne me traduit . . .

Énigmes de la vie et de la connaissance!
les deux arbres au même jardin.

Et vous vous ruez dans la parole sans douter d'elle,
dans la pensée, comme si elle pouvait résoudre la vie!

Les deux arbres issus de la même terre
et retournant à elle avec leurs fruits.

Restez simples si vous êtes possédés par le démon de dire,
si vous ne pouvez rien contre lui.

Toujours plus simples, au cours de vos croissances!
un peu plus d'altitude ne vous fournira rien.

Appelez-en au Christ pour porter votre drame,
au Christ de l'agonie et de la remise de l'esprit.

Les deux arbres issus de la même lumière
et retournant à elle avec leurs fruits!

Dans vos retournements restez toujours des pauvres,
mendiez obstinément de la parole de Dieu.

PSALM 14

So you claim to speak of the tragedy within you?
you forget that speaking itself is an enigma.

That emptiness you suffer from murmurs only:
no word can translate me . . .

Enigmas of life and knowledge:
they are like two trees in the same garden.

And you fling yourself into words without doubting them,
into thought, as if it could make sense of living!

They are two trees issued from the same earth
to which they return their fruits.

If you are possessed by the demon of speech,
if you cannot resist him,

strive to remain simple.
A higher register will furnish you nothing.

Call out to Christ to carry your drama,
to the Christ of agony and of the spirit's deliverance.

They are like two trees issued from the same light
to which they return their fruits.

Remain impoverished from your returns,
like beggars asking stubbornly for God's word.

Sinon vos voix s'empêtreront dans les filets du langage,
vos âmes dans les méandres de la pensée.

Et laissez vous mener vers le jardin de l'avenir:
la lumière porte son secret.

Otherwise your voices will tangle in language's threads,
your souls in thought's meanderings.

And let yourself be led toward a future garden:
light carries its secret.

PSAUME 16

Ne fera-t-il pas partie du chœur parce que sa chair le domine,
parce qu'il se cache parfois de nous pour faire l'amour?

Il arrive devant l'autel avec des yeux fatigués,
un regard encombré par des souvenirs d'étreinte.

Il dit: Comment chanterais-je le Seigneur?
toute une part de mon cœur n'est pas tournée vers lui.

Alors comme si nous lui reprochions ses jouissances,
il se retourne avec violence contre tes chanteurs.

Il nous traite de faussaires en amour,
il invective le chœur qui trie ainsi ses voix.

Il se refuse à l'examen d'entrée de ta louange,
il la chantonne malgré lui.

Il cherche aussi le monde d'amour, Seigneur,
dans le trouble où il fraye son sentier.

Quel chœur ne ferais-tu avec tous ces pécheurs,
leur pudeur à te célébrer?

PSALM 16

Will he not join in the choir because his flesh controls him,
because sometimes he disappears to go make love?

He shows up before the altar with tired eyes
and a faraway look toward last night's embrace.

He says: How could I sing to the Lord?
an entire part of my heart is turned away from him.

And as if we had reproached him for his pleasures,
he comes back at your singers with violence.

He treats our affections like forgeries, hurls abuse
at a choir who'd select such voices.

He won't permit himself to try the first words of the song,
but despite himself he hums along.

He also is seeking love's realm, Lord,
in the agitation with which he makes his own path.

What sort of choir do you make with all these sinners,
their embarrassment to celebrate you?

PSAUME 17

Pas seulement sous mes pieds, la terre!
ma tête, mes yeux eux-mêmes en sont pétris.

Et ce n'est pas au loin que j'écoute sa plainte,
mais à la chair de mes oreilles, à mon esprit.

Quand ma voix te rend grâce, mon Dieu,
c'est une gorge de terre qui la rend.

Les eaux qui ravinent ma gorge ne sont pas pures,
elles charrient tous mes sens en dévalant.

Ceux qui ne cherchent pas leur vraie voix sans relâche
ignorent mon trouble, mon obsession.

Dangereux est le chemin que je fraye, Seigneur,
mortel peut-être dans mes illusions.

Mais en cette vie recluse, je te cherche quand même!
ma quête est insensée, rassure-moi.

Si orgueilleuse que puisse être l'enquête,
si fatale que soit la chute de ma voix,

Ne me laisse pas tomber dans un gouffre d'air rare,
ni étouffer au sol que tu travailles d'en bas.

PSALM 17

It's not just under my feet, the earth—
even my eyes, my head are filled with it.

And it's not from a distance that I hear its groan,
but from my ear's own flesh, from my mind.

When my voice delivers praise, my God,
it issues from a throat of clay.

Furrowed by waters that are not pure,
gushing down with all my senses.

Those who do not restlessly seek their true voice
understand neither my turmoil nor obsession.

It's a dangerous path I clear to reach you,
deadly perhaps in my illusions.

But in this life of solitude, I nevertheless seek you.
My quest is foolish. Comfort me.

As arrogant as this investigation might be,
as fatal my voice's failing,

don't let me plummet into an abyss of rarified air
or suffocate in the soil you turn below.

PSAUME 18

Il paraît que j'ai peur de vivre parce que je trouve un refuge
loins des remous de surface, à mon creux.

Je n'ai pas travaillé à durcir mon écorce:
ah! le coeur de mon bois est bien plus tumultueux!

Il ne suinte pas dès qu'on l'effleure,
mais se verse d'un coup sous d'autres vents.

C'est pourquoi j'ai si peu de compassion aux lèvres,
ma quête n'a pas de sens à qui m'attend.

Mon refuge lui paraît un confort,
ma retraite, un aveu de lâcheté.

Mais ta grâce, Seigneur, abandonne-t-elle les lâches?
la connaissent-ils, ceux qui me jugent d'un regard?

Ont-ils pesé l'obsession de dire
et le poids de se croire chargé de ce devoir?

Comment leur décrirai-je tous ces vents qu'ils ignorent
et ce coeur submergé par les marées du sang?

Comment leur montrerai-je que certains vents s'y forment,
des courants, des contre-courants?

Je m'acharne par force à traduire l'ineffable:
ma version de la vie ne parviendra jamais à la clarté.

PSALM 18

Because I take refuge far from the wuthering surface,
in my hollow, it looks like I'm afraid of life.

I've made no attempt to toughen my bark exterior:
oh, the heart inside the wood is so much more tumultuous.

If you scrape against the surface, nothing bleeds out,
but some gusts make all the sap spill at once.

That's why I have so little compassion at my lips,
there's no way to know what, in the end, is waiting for me.

My refuge appears too comfortable to him,
my withdrawal, an admission of cowardice.

But does your grace, Lord, abandon cowards?
Do they know that, those who judge me at a glance?

Have they felt the weight of the obsession to speak
and the burden of believing one is charged with such a task?

How will I describe these unpredictable gusts
and show them this heart submerged in waves of blood?

How will I show them that wind forms itself
into currents, then counter-currents?

I waste my efforts translating the ineffable:
my rendering of life will never achieve clarity.

Qui pourra croire à mes cavernes, à mes arbres?
qui prendra mes pierres pour vraies?

Who would believe in my caverns, in my trees?
who will take my stones for real?

PSAUME 20

Quand tu apaises mon coeur, je n'ai plus rien à dire,
les mots inquiets qui me remuent tombent endormis.

Je ne sens même plus mon drame de créature:
ta berceuse m'amène au jour, pas au sommeil.

On m'assure que c'est un mirage des sens,
que la plaie de mon cœur doit rester vive devant toi.

Parce qu'il faut que l'angoisse des autres la ravive,
parce qu'il n'est pas bon d'étouffer leur rumeur.

Ils n'ont pas tort, tu me viens aussi pars leurs bouches,
mais qu'ils ne touchent pas à ton aube sur ma vie!

Cette aube où tout est pris dans ton adoration quelques secondes,
et puis tu reviens d'ailleurs, tu reviens d'eux et de leur nuit.

PSALM 20

When you appease my heart, I've nothing left to say,
my agitated words fall fast asleep.

I don't even remember my petty dramas—
your lullaby sings me awake.

Others assure me I imagine this, that to receive you
the wound in my chest must stay fresh.

And that the anguish of others reopens the cut,
and that it's not good to suppress their clamor.

It's not that they're wrong, you come to me this way, too,
but don't let them touch your dawn upon my life,

Those few seconds of dawn when everything is taken with adoration,
and you come back from elsewhere, you return from someone else's darkness.

PSAUME 21

A m'entendre chanter mes chaumes, mes collines,
on me dit: C'est un jeu!

Occupe ta vie à dessiner ton pays d'âme,
mais ne vise pas le plus sérieux.

Ton Dieu est comme tes vanneaux ou tes ormes:
on te scrute, il n'y a rien.

Mon Dieu, ne me laisse pas sans réponse:
toi que je cherche n'es pas rien.

Je le sais bien que mon assise n'est pas ferme,
mais quel est l'homme qui ne s'élève sur un creux?

Ceux qui le cachent travaillent sur artifice,
c'est leur réseau d'idées qui est un jeu.

Je chante sans filet pour amortir ma chute,
la seule reprise de mon souffle me maintient.

Il s'en prend à un vol de vanneaux sur les chaumes,
et mon cœur bat si fort qu'il le fait sien.

Au couple d'ormes isolé sur la colline,
et le voici en moi, sur mon chemin.

Ma quête peut n'être rien pour les experts,
pour moi, c'est ton approche par ta création.

PSALM 21

When they hear me sing my stubble fields, my little hills,
they tell me: It's make-believe!

Spending your life drawing your own soul's country,
unconcerned with what's most serious.

Your God is like your lapwings or elms:
scanning the horizon, one finds nothing there.

My God, don't leave me without a response:
you whom I seek are not nothing.

I know all too well my footing's unstable,
but where is the man who doesn't straddle an abyss?

Those who hide this fact labor on artifice,
it's their network of ideas that is "make-believe."

I sing without even a thread to cushion my fall,
only the repetition of my breath supports me.

It pauses for a flight of lapwings above the bare fields
and my heart beats so hard it thinks it's flying.

At the pair of elm trees isolated upon the hill,
there he is, with me on my path.

My quest may be nothing to the experts,
but for me, it's to approach him by his own creation.

Il y a bien des couches dans l'épaisseur de l'homme,
et mon Dieu est le Dieu de leur procréation.

A travers mon esprit, il travaille l'argile,
et tout ce qui s'élève d'elle dit son Nom.

There are many layers in the depths of man,
and my God is the God who made them.

Through my spirit, he works the clay
and everything that rises from it speaks his Name.

PSAUME 22

Il y a des étoiles dans mon ciel que l'on ne voit pas à l'oeil nu,
dans ma nuit privé, je les nomme.

Comme l'espèce l'a fait pour les grands astres,
je les fixe, je leur donne des noms.

Mon ciel de nuit ne change guère,
j'avance dans le temps et elles sont toujours là.

Comme un devin, je dis les bonnes, les mauvaises,
comme un juge qui fait crédit à son jugement.

A leur clarté, je vois rôder des formes sur ma terre,
des bêtes qui ne sortent qu'au soir tombant.

Je dis encore les bonnes, les nuisibles,
comme un penseur qui se classe lui-même parmi les innocents.

Et puis brusquement, je dois me taire,
toute ma faune, toutes mes étoiles en fumée.

Seigneur, la vocation d'un poète est tragique,
surtout lorsque pour toi il veut tout renouveler.

Et lorsqu'il prend de ta parole pour comprendre,
ce qu'il en fait scintille un moment et s'abat.

Le vent chasse comme des nuages ses poèmes,
il envoie son esprit au monde, et son esprit ne revient pas.

PSALM 22

In my sky there are stars invisible to the naked eye
and alone at night, I name them.

I arrange them, I give them names
from a taxonomy invented for the great stars.

My night sky hardly changes—the stars
remain fixed while I move through time.

I'm the one who determines which ones are good, which bad,
like a judge who finds his own rulings final.

By starlight, I can just begin to see the roaming bodies
of the nocturnal creatures who first appear at dusk.

Again I say which are good, which are bothersome,
just like a thinker who classifies himself among the innocent.

And then abruptly I have no choice but silence
as all my fauna, all my stars turn to smoke.

Lord, the vocation of a poet is tragic,
especially when he wants to make everything new for you.

And when he uses your words to understand,
whatever he makes sparkles for an instant and falls away.

He sends out his spirit to the world, and his spirit does not come back.
Like wind chasing clouds, his poems disappear.

Il reste face à face avec la seule question: Pourquoi faire?
et puis la vie insiste en disant: Tu feras.

Mais toi, le Seigneur de la vie, dis-tu de même?
tout vacille, le soir s'étend . . . est-ce toi?

He remains face to face with the only question: *Why do this?*
and then life insists, saying: *You will.*

But you, the Lord of life, is that what you say?
everything sways, the night stretches out—is it you?

PSAUME 23

Les mers lointaines ne connaissent pas mon visage,
et moi, je chante obstinément la mer.

Mon jardin suffit-il à parler de la terre?
à peine ai-je mis le pied à l'étranger.

Mon ambition secrète est trop risible!
et moi seul n'en ris pas tout à fait.

Je la confesse à voix haute pour m'en défaire:
mon Dieu, elle resurgit d'ailleurs, sitôt jetée.

Elle dit aux arbres: vous n'êtes pas hors de ma prise,
je tiens du mystère végétal comme vous.

Aux animaux des fonds de forêts ou de mer:
l'homme ne vous contient-il pas tous?

Et à vous que je n'ai jamais vus dans mon ciel, vous les anges,
vous tairai-je comme si vous n'y passiez pas?

J'élève dans ma voix un corps de poésie,
j'exhale tout ce qui me peuple dans mon souffle.

Qu'on m'objecte: ce n'est qu'une bulle d'air en forme de monde!
je réponds: que m'importe si elle éclate au vent?

Que m'importe si d'autres souffles humains la crèvent?
elle se reformera dans ton adoration.

PSALM 23

Faraway seas have never seen my face,
and yet I sing obstinately of the sea.

Does my garden suffice to speak about the earth?
I have hardly stepped a foot beyond it.

I am the only one who doesn't find
my secret ambition ridiculous.

I admit it out loud in order to cure myself
but my God, it resurfaces each time I reject it.

It says to the trees: you are not beyond my grasp,
I hold vegetal mystery like you.

To the animals deep in the forest or the sea:
man does not contain all of you within himself?

And to you whom I have never glimpsed above, you angels,
should I keep quiet about you as if you weren't there?

With my voice I raise up a body made of poetry,
I exhale in my breath everything that populates me.

If one objects: it's nothing but an air bubble shaped like the world!
I respond: what does it matter if it bursts in the wind?

What does it matter if it's punctured by another human breath?
It will reshape itself in adoration of you.

PSAUME 24

Depuis toujours j'ai comme un poids sous ma conscience,
chaque fois que je veux danser, je le ressens.

Il ne me rabat pas seulement vers la terre,
mais au secret de toute la terre dont j'ai un champ.

J'ai beau me reposer sur ce champ, sur moi-même:
moi-même se dérobe et s'évanouit.

Dans une nuit plus vaste que la mienne,
comme une semence infime, je suis blotti.

Tout est encore à recommencer, dis-je au Seigneur,
car là, je parle à Dieu en familier.

Tout de la croissance et de la reproduction est à rapprendre!
ta grâce de pesanteur me fait le découvrir.

Un plus lourd secret que le mien me travaille,
il suinte de mon sol, je ne peux le tenir.

Du plus obscur un reflet semble naître,
un reflet à reprendre par ton jour plus tard.

Qu'on ne me mette pas au rang des visionnaires!
rien dans ce reflet ne se laisse voir.

Mais je fais mon poème comme un frêne ses feuilles:
pas la lumière, un frêne n'en fait pas.

PSALM 24

I've always felt something like a weight just beneath my awareness—
whenever I want to dance, I can feel it.

It lowers me not only toward the ground but deep
into an earth-sized secret—where I have a field.

How I love to lie down in this field—in myself:
myself in hiding, then disappearing.

Into a night vaster than my own,
sinking into it like a miniscule seed.

Everything can start over, I tell the Lord,
for there, I speak to God in familiar terms.

How to grow and how to increase be relearned—
the grace of your gravity presses me to discover.

A secret heavier than my own weighs on me,
it seeps out of my soil, I can't keep it.

From utter darkness a glimmering begins,
the kind of glimmer your daylight will later contain.

No one could count me among the visionaries!
Nothing in this dimness allows itself to be seen.

I make my poems the way an ash tree makes leaves—
not light, that's not for an ash tree to do.

Je t'en supplie, Seigneur, joue sur mes feuilles,
avant de me reprendre tout entier chez toi.

Before you take me back entirely, Lord, I ask you kindly:
dapple light upon my leaves.

PSAUME 25

Tu m'as alloué trop de bonheurs, mon Dieu!
comment en répondrai-je devant toi?

Ma part de souffrance est futile,
et je n'ai pas le cœur de te prier de l'alourdir.

Tu m'as alloué une vocation de parole,
mais elle ne peut aller jusque-là.

Elle butine de la douleur du monde:
ah! c'est moins lourd que d'en être la proie!

Je me creuse pour que vie et parole s'accordent,
je m'épuise pour leur trouver un même cœur.

Mais il s'obstine vers la joie, mon sacrifice,
il ne me presse guère de renoncer à mes bonheurs.

Je regarde ton Christ et je m'affole,
mes privilèges sont trop lourds à porter.

Ce n'est pas d'être heureux qui me mine,
mais l'angoisse du scandale à parler du Seigneur.

On me jette: non, tu ne portes pas son signe,
tu t'enterres pour ne pas te blesser au dehors!

Mais moi, je n'y peux rien que je croie à ta grâce,
et qu'une joie obscure tressaille sous mon bonheur.

PSALM 25

You allotted me too much happiness, my God!
how will I answer for this before you?

My portion of suffering is trivial
and I don't have the heart to ask you to increase it.

You allotted me the vocation of speaking,
but that doesn't go far enough.

It gleans pain from the world:
but that's less heavy than being prey to it!

I empty myself so that life and word will align,
I exhaust myself to locate them in the same heart.

But it insists its way toward joy, and my sacrifice
hardly presses me to relinquish my happiness.

I look at your Christ and am terrified,
my privileges are too heavy to bear.

It's not being happy that eats away at me,
but the anguish of the scandal of even speaking about the Lord.

One could say: no, you are not carrying sign of him,
you're burying your own self so as not to be hurt from the outside!

I can't help it if I can only believe in your grace,
if beneath my happiness shudders a dark joy.

PSAUME 26

Ils me lisent, et puis s'interrogent:
que sommes-nous venus faire ici?

Ici, c'est le domaine de mon souffle et lui-même,
je l'expire, j'expire mon esprit.

Alors l'un d'eux montre la bête naïve qui le mène,
une bête qui se plaît aux berceuses de ma voix.

Un autre dit: j'ai eu vent d'une formation nouvelle,
mais le vent a tourné, elle ne tient pas.

Un autre: j'espérais entendre ce qui me manque:
me voici un peu triste, mais rassuré.

Moi, j'écoute une voix derrière celles qui m'entourent,
celle qui vient de derrière moi s'y reconnaît.

C'est un souffle plutôt qui ne passe pas au langage,
je pose même un doigt sur ma bouche pour l'arrêter.

Il se glisse à travers mes lèvres closes,
impossible de le rattraper, il murmure Dieu.

Il ne passe pas aux mots, pourtant il s'y infiltre,
il charge de silence chacun d'eux.

PSALM 26

They read me and then ask themselves:
what did we come here for?

"Here" is the realm of my breath and this self
I exhale, my spirit that I exhale.

One of them will point to the animal that led him here,
a dumb creature pleased by the lullabies of my voice.

Another will say: *I felt the wind of something new,*
but then the wind changed, the something didn't stay.

And another: *I wanted to understand what I am missing,*
now I'm a little sad but reassured.

Me, I hear a voice behind those around me,
one that comes up from behind me and clearly knows the way.

It's almost a breath—it doesn't travel by language—
I even hold a finger up to my mouth to stop it.

It glides through my closed lips,
impossible to recapture. It murmurs God.

It doesn't move through words, but it seeps into them,
filling each one with silence.

PSAUME 29

Venez dans mes sentiers si vous avez perdu les vôtres,
suivez-les quelques pas, et puis allez frayer vos chemins.

Car c'est en tâtonnant que j'avance dans l'ombre,
je n'assure jamais le matin.

Changez le nom des arbres que je cite sur ma route,
dites-la de sable ou d'argile selon vos sols.

Nuancez le ciel avec les nuages qui montent de vos mers,
ne vous prenez pas pour des oiseaux de haut vol.

Ne croyez pas à moi, à ma parole,
croyez à ce qui cherche en nous le Seigneur.

Écoutez les noms d'approche que je lui trouve,
mais ne les retenez que s'ils suscitent votre cri.

Sauf pour adorer le Seigneur,
ne prenez pas vos distances avec lui.

N'écrasez pas en vous ce qui murmure son nom avec confiance,
lui-même l'a semé parmi vos éléments.

C'est un germe qui a besoin de sa lumière pour la croissance,
pour devenir une réponse du sang.

PSALM 29

If you have lost your way, come over to my path,
follow it a few steps, but then go clear your own.

Because it's only by groping in the dark that I make my way,
I am never certain of morning's return.

Change the name of the trees I cite on my route,
call it sand or clay according to your ground.

Be specific about the clouds that rise above your seas,
don't just assume they're shadows of flying birds.

Don't believe in me or in my words,
believe in whatever is in us that seeks the Lord.

Listen to the words I find for him,
but retain them only if they arouse your own cry.

Except as a way to love the Lord,
do not keep your distance from him.

Do not crush what confidently whispers his name inside you,
for he, himself, is planted among your elements.

It's a growing seed that needs his light
to become an answer in the blood.

PSAUME 30

Ici, et sans poser la pierre terminale,
je poserai déjà mon testament.

Mais qui parle de pierre? Pas de voûte à mon livre!
rien qu'une baie ouverte au vent.

Déjà je veux donner sa note comme la dernière,
le concert pas encore sur ses fins.

Aie pitié, Seigneur, de mon chant téméraire,
remets-moi tout le devoir que j'oublie.

A certains donateurs, je voudrais un peu rendre,
souffler le retour de l'esprit.

A ce confident d'intelligence, le pari de mon intelligence,
à ce coureur du large, la chasse sur mes plateaux étroits.

A celui qui m'a provoqué, cet espoir de genèse,
à celui qui s'est tu, le silence de ma voix.

A celle qui s'est livrée à toi, ma retraite,
à ceux qui ne t'ont pas entendu, l'appel que tu m'as fait.

A cette âme de riche, ma prière d'impuissance,
à cet esprit du froid, mon feu presque étouffé.

Car beaucoup m'ont donné, qui l'ignorent encore,
et ma langue ne peut pas tous te les nommer.

PSALM 30

Here, and without placing the final stone,
I will set down already my testament.

But who said stone? There's no archway for my book!
nothing but an opening to the wind.

Already I want to deliver its note as final,
the concert not quite ended.

Have pity, Lord, on my reckless song,
put before me the tasks I am forgetting.

To certain donors, I would like to give back
a little, to blow the spirit's return.

And to this confidant, the wager of my intelligence,
to this runner of expanse, the run of my limited plateaus.

To the one who provoked me, this hope of genesis,
to the one who keep quiet, the silence of my voice.

To the one who surrendered herself to you, my retreat,
to those who didn't understand, the call that you made to me.

To the soul of wealth, my prayer of weakness,
to this spirit of coldness, my almost extinguished fire.

For so many, still unaware of it, gave to me,
and my tongue cannot name them all for you.

En un seul nom, Seigneur, je les résume,
je les serre et le tien s'étend.

Qu'ils prennent patience, ceux qui te cherchent!
est-ce que je ne te cherche pas encore?

Qu'ils veillent, ceux qui assurent ne pas te reconnaître!
est-ce que je te connais?

Oui, je me suis peut-être enfoui trop en moi-même,
mais eux et toi, je vous ai retrouvés là.

Alors que ce testament les ramène à leur grâce:
ce qui m'est vital, c'est toi.

In a single word, Lord, I aim to collect them,
I hold them tight as your hand extends.

May they practice patience, those who seek you!
don't I myself still seek you?

May they be on watch, those who claim not to recognize you!
do I recognize you?

Yes, perhaps I am a little too buried in myself,
but you, them, that's where I found you all again.

May this testament lead them to your grace:
what's vital to me is you.

PSAUME 31

Celui qui voulait trop comprendre,
tu l'as frappé sans cesse au sens d'être compris:
pour un Seigneur, tu rabats fort quand tu commandes!

Il ne te défait pas avec l'intelligence,
il ne faisait que te tendre ses branches:
tu pèses lourd pour un Dieu de lumière!

Tu n'as pas foudroyé sa tête,
mais crevé le sol sous ses pieds:
ah! tu veux qu'il déchante! as-tu gagné?

Je t'avais réservé pourtant toute altitude,
je ne me dressais pas au vide, mais vers toi:
as-tu gagné, Seigneur, à ce jeu-là?

La vie cherche l'essor et non pas le décours;
mon Dieu vivant, n'aurais-tu pas perdu?
et qui rira lorsque ma foi n'en pourra plus?

Mais l'homme trop rétif à sortir de lui-même,
tu l'y enfonces comme un oiseau,
qu'il aille débrider la plaie de son baptême.

Par les veines et non les artères,
vers la terre promise au-dessous de ses terres,
le désert et le cœur des eaux.

PSALM 31

The one who wanted to understand too much,
you struck him endlessly to be understood:
for a Lord, you come down hard when you decide to.

He wasn't defying your intelligence,
he was only stretching his branches up to you:
you weigh so heavy for a God of light.

You didn't strike his head with lightning
but hollowed the ground beneath his feet instead:
oh, how you tried to disenchant him. Did you win?

I had reserved, however, every height as yours,
I wasn't addressing the void, but you:
have you won this little game, Lord?

Life seeks to increase, not to diminish;
my living God, haven't you lost?
Who will laugh once my faith's exhausted?

But the man too stubborn to go beyond himself,
you cut into him like a bird,
you christen him by peeling back his wound,

going not through arteries but into the veins,
down into the holy ground underneath his ground,
into the desert and the water's source.

Et tout au long, ton rire à la place du ciel:
que l'oiseau migrateur s'abatte enfin sur elles,
que l'arbre se retourne enfin!

Seigneur, seul Appelant à la vocation d'homme,
aie pitié de ce nom que mes lèvres te forment,
et ne m'appelle plus de mon nom, mais du tien!

And all the while there's your laugh where the sky should be:
to make the migrating bird swoop down to the water,
to make the tree finally come back.

Lord, sole Plaintiff for the human vocation,
have pity for this name my lips form of you
and don't summon me by my name, but by yours.

PSAUME 32

N'ai-je pas droit, Seigneur, à des saisons?
n'as-tu pas fait erreur en ce trop long hiver?
mon âme cherche en vain òu s'accoupler.

Je n'anime plus rien et tout me désanime,
ma voix me revient morte au moindre appel vers toi!
peut-être en veux-tu à ma voix.

Sans elle je ne suis qu'un cavalier sans ma monture,
un poète perdu pour ta benediction:
j'ai dû vouloir forcer ta grace.

Plus sommaire est mon cri que celui de tes bêtes,
la moindre pierre est plus musicienne que moi,
ma gorge désolée s'encrasse . . .

Descelle-moi, mon Dieu, je me meurs d'être atone:
depuis trois ans, je me défonce, je me fore,
je m'entends gémir. . . . M'entends-tu?

J'ai quitté pour toi des terres profanes
et ton silence me condamne!
non, je ne réclame pas mon dû!

Mais au moins penche-toi, ne laisse pas s'étendre
sur ma quête un ciel d'indifférence,
ne me laisse pas égorgé . . .

PSALM 32

Don't I have a right, Lord, to the seasons?
haven't you made an error with this too long winter?
my soul looks in vain for something to attach to.

Nothing enlivens me anymore and I bring nothing to life,
my voice returns hollow from the smallest call for you.
Perhaps it's my voice you despise.

I had tried to seize your grace:
without it I am just a cavalier with no mount,
a poet stranded without your blessing.

Even a rock is more musician than me,
my cry is less articulate than a beast's,
my sorry throat fouls everything up . . .

Stop me, my God, from atoning myself to death:
for three years I've broken myself, I've bored into myself,
I hear the sound of my own moans—do you hear me?

I left the realm of the profane behind for you
and now you condemn me with silence.
No, I have not received my due!

At least, come down to me. Don't extend
an indifferent sky above me,
don't leave me with a throat slit open . . .

PSAUME 33

Tu m'assèches, tu me dépeuples, tu me creuses,
comme si tu voulais que je fusse une tombe
plus morte que son mort, mais que son mort fût toi . . .

Dieu qui d'un homme assis fais lever un nomade,
est-ce á toi que j'ai obéi?
J'aimais plus simplement lorsque j'étais petit.

Ma voix te bénissait dans ses bonheurs de dire!
Est-ce ta grâce? est-ce mon mal qui la déchire?
je ne sais même plus qui la torture ainsi.

Si c'est encore à toi que je crie mon angoisse,
je m'écoeure à l'entendre haletante et si basse:
mon battement de coeur n'est-il plus que ton glas?

Si je te crois encore le confident plus proche,
si je rêve toujours de chanter pour tes noces,
est-ce par habitude ou par amour de toi?

Pourquoi m'avoir chargé d'un tel désir de louange
si c'était pour me changer d'ange,
me confier à celui qui doit écarteler?

Encore si j'y voyais le sceau de ta souffrance,
si dans ton agonie je pouvais battre au sens
d'être brisé à mort pour mieux te ressembler!

PSALM 33

You make a drought in me, you depopulate me, you leave me
hollow enough to be the tomb that housed his death,
his death that was all your doing . . .

God who turns a settled man into a wanderer:
you're the one I used to obey?
I loved you more simply when I was young.

My voice once praised you so happily!
Was that your grace? Is it now my wrong who breaks it?
I no longer know who's the tormentor.

If it's still to you that I cry out my anguish,
I'm sickened by the halting realization:
isn't it you who tolls my heart like a funeral bell?

If it's still you I confide in most intimately,
if I still dream of singing your nuptials,
is it from habit or actual love for you?

Why did you burden me with such a desire to praise
before you made me an angel,
why invest in someone who must be torn apart?

If only I understood your suffering, if only I could
strike down my sense of being broken to death
the better to resemble you.

Mais j'ai peur de tricher et d'aggraver ma dette . . .
tu n'es pas Dieu à demander ma tête
et qu'ai-je d'autre pour payer?

But I'm afraid to cheat and worsen my debt . . .
a God like you wouldn't ask for my head
and yet what else do I have to pay with?

PSAUME 35

Mon plus profond désir: parler de toi;
ma hantise: te compromettre!
je ne parlerai plus qu'à toi.

Tant pis pour ma croissance dans ce siècle!
il parle, sans veiller le mystère de dire,
il pense, mais sans croire aux noces de l'esprit!

Tu m'as mené dans cet exode:
quand j'entrevois son terme, il recule d'autant!
donne-moi l'eau avant le feu, mon Christ brûlant!

Si je t'élève une prière exaspérée
de n'être qu'un cri d'impuissance,
si je ne rends plus grâce, entends ce que je tais.

Et si plus rien de moi n'aspire
à cette quête à ciel perdu,
écoute ma fatigue et non pas mon refus.

Est-il encor très loin, ton lieu de grâce?
mes démons se relaient pour m'étreindre à ta place,
ils m'offrent des miroirs où je lis ma folie!

Brouille-les, mon Christ, toi qui m'aimes,
je ne veux pas me contempler moi-même,
je cherche ta face et ta vie.

PSALM 35

My most profound desire: to speak of you;
my shame: to compromise you!
So I will speak only to you.

Too bad for me, believing in you in this century
that speaks, without keeping vigil on the mystery of speaking,
that thinks, without believing in the marriage of the spirit!

You led me in this exodus:
when I glimpse its end, it draws back!
give me water before you give me fire, my burning Christ!

If I raise an exasperated prayer
of not being anything more than a powerless cry,
if I no longer praise you, understand what I keep silent.

And if nothing in me aspires any longer
to this quest toward a lost heaven,
hear my fatigue, not my refusal.

Is your place of grace still very far to reach?
my demons take turns holding me in your place,
they offer me mirrors in which I read my own madness!

Disorient them, my Christ who loves me,
I don't want to contemplate myself all alone,
I am looking for your countenance and your life.

Avant mon terme, avant que je ne meure . . .
oui, l'exode vers toi avant mon heure:
c'est la tienne toujours: tu l'as dit.

Où passe Dieu, je passerai, mais s'il me porte,
l'aventure est gagnée, s'il gagne mes eaux mortes,
les mots de son amour franchissent tout en lui.

Before my ending, before I die . . .
yes, the exodus toward you before my last hour:
it's always yours: as you said.

Where God goes, I will go, but if he carries me,
the adventure is won, if he conquers my still waters,
if his love's words cross over everything in him.

PSAUME 36

Mon démon a repris sa hargne,
il me harcèle comme un sexe adolescent,
me tord comme jamais ne m'a tordu mon sang!

Ni l'âge ne l'a fait céder, ni ce voyage:
il renaît plus violent des longues continences . . .
ah! ne saisir qu'en desserrant l'intelligence!

J'ai fait un pas de trop, et dans quel piège!
je te cherchais des noms: comment t'appellerai-je
si c'est toujours à contre-moi que tu me veux?

Comme une bête prise, je me déchire,
je bave du blasphème entre mes dents,
je me défends goutte à goutte de sang.

Reviens-moi: à mon coeur il est place pour deux . . .
qui parle ainsi, moi ou mon Dieu?
que ma voix réponde à la sienne!

Reviens-moi: à ton coeur il est place pour tout!
goutte à goutte mon sang se perd et m'y ramène,
se perd et se refait dans ton règne au-dessous.

Quoi! la sève affleurant au ras de la pensée
et refluant au coeur, c'était pour annoncer
d'autres noms pour mon Dieu!

PSALM 36

My demon has turned surly again,
he torments me like a sex-starved teenager,
twists me ways my flesh has never been perverted.

He doesn't yield to age, nor to this pursuit:
he only surfaces more violently during long self-restraint,
seizing me only to undo my intelligence.

I took one step too far—and into what a trap!
I was searching for names to call you: and what should I call
you who always seems to want me self-divided?

Now I tear at myself like a trapped animal—
blasphemy foaming between my teeth—
as I defend myself with each drop of blood.

Come back to me: in my heart there is room for two . . .
Who speaks this, me or my God?
May it be my voice answering his!

Come back to me: in your heart there is room for everything!
drop by drop my blood drains and carries me away,
drains and refreshes in your kingdom below.

It's sap running over thought's surface
and flowing back down into the heart
to announce other names for my God.

Tu es le méprisé des grands règnes de vie,
au plus bas, au plus sourd avec ton Christ enfoui,
et mon cri révolté devient d'un amoureux . . .

You are the most scorned of life's great rulers,
the lowest, the most muted with your buried Christ:
now my outraged cry becomes that of a lover's . . .

PSAUME 37

Ah! l'aube . . . et ce premier printemps sur l'hiver nu
où toi seul pouvais être ami, toi seulement
disais encore la vie quand tout était mourant!

Il n'était que ta bouche à défier l'évidence,
et je m'y suspendais comme pour un baiser,
je t'appelais amour quand tu désenchantais.

Ma sincérité même allait à la dérive:
tu me laissais forger ta promesse pour vivre,
tu me laissais crier sans la joie de bénir.

Mon cantique est tombé comme vaine parure:
oui, tu m'as dénudé jusqu'à le refuser,
même mon cri de bête est tombé au murmure.

Tu ne m'as concédé qu'un règne, qu'un seul règne
comme signe du tien, mais de si peu de vie:
un brin d'herbe dans la désolation humaine.

Tout peut-il se reprendre et s'élever de lui?
quoi? le fameux abîme à notre intelligence,
le fameux vide humain n'était que son silence?

Ah! l'aube, ton regard sur ma nuit végétale,
ce tout petit frisson en attente du vent . . .
voudras-tu me confier une voix de printemps?

PSALM 37

Dawn! . . . and spring's first touch on naked winter
when you alone could be my friend, only you
still spoke of life while everything was dying!

There was only your mouth to defy the evidence,
and I suspended myself there as if waiting for a kiss.
I called you love while you dispelled charm.

Even my sincerity went adrift:
you let me mold your promise of life,
you let me shout without the joy of your blessing.

Then my hymn fell like a useless costume:
yes, you stripped it off me
until my animal moaning fell to a murmur.

All you've granted me is a kingdom, a single kingdom
symbolic of your own but with so little life:
a blade of grass in the human desolation.

Can anything just decide to grow upward and reach him?
Is the gaping abyss in our knowledge—
this gaping human emptiness—just his silence?

Ah, dawn, your gaze upon my earthly night,
this tiny shiver anticipating wind . . .
won't you confide in me a voice of spring?

PSAUME 41

Mon Dieu, je ne sais que ma dette,
toute ma vie portée en dette,
et toi qui la remets d'un mot!

Pardonne-moi mon impudence:
toi qui m'enserrais de partout,
délivre-moi pour ton dimanche.

Remets en cours ton ciel nocturne,
retisse des constellations
comme des supports à ta louange.

Le jour où tu vérifieras
le goût de mes joies à tes lèvres,
de ma tristesse à ta Passion,

Pourras-tu dire: c'est un homme
qui n'a pas voulu m'échanger
contre trente idées lumineuses!

PSALM 41

My God, I know only my debt,
all my life carried in debt,
and you who repays it in a word!

Forgive me my shamelessness:
you who have endlessly carried me,
deliver me in time for your day of rest.

Reset the night sky in motion,
reweave the constellations
into a net for your praise.

On that day when you decide,
when all my joy is tasted on your lips,
my sadness at your Passion,

will you say: here is a man
who valued me
over thirty radiant ideas?

PSAUME 42

Tu ne m'avais pas dit qu'il serait si terrible
de te chercher en moi . . . tu ne m'avais pas dit
qu'il te serait si dur de m'avoir pour ami!

N'en ai-je pas fini d'attendre ta lumière?
garde-moi une part à sa profusion,
si c'est possible, ô Dieu, ma part de création.

Mais tiens-moi ferme en mon insuffisance:
tu pourvois à ton espérance,
toi seul es ma vocation.

Mène-moi plus profond t'entendre dans ta nuit,
mais n'oublie pas mon vieux pari avec le monde:
je t'ai promis le jeu de l'homme devant lui.

Il m'attend aux épreuves de haute montagne:
ai-je appris les rappels savants sur les arêtes?
je ne sais que ton nom jusqu'au fond de l'ennui.

Le désert reprend sur ton ordre:
il n'est pas fini, mon exode!
tiens ma mémoire jusqu'au bout.

Je ne te verrai que plus tard:
tu es la lumière du soir,
alors tu découvriras tout.

PSALM 42

You never told me it would be so terrible
to look inside myself . . . you never said
how hard it would be to have me as a friend!

Am I still not finished waiting for your light?
O God, keep one part of its profusion,
if possible, for me.

And in my inadequacy, hold me close:
provide me your hope,
be my only vocation.

Lead me deeper into your night so I can hear you,
but don't forget my old wager with the world:
I promised to illustrate man's play to himself.

Trials await me high in the mountains:
on the ridges will I recall the wise men's reminders?
in the depths of ennui I know only your name.

The desert takes your order up again:
my exodus is not over!
keep hold of my memory until the end.

Only much later will I get to see you,
the light in the darkness
that reveals each thing.

PSAUME 45

Pas seulement mes mots, c'est moi que tu attends,
c'est moi, ton mot, que je te rends:
avant de parler, j'étais dit.

Noie de ton ombre mes vallées
comme tu fis à mes hauteurs:
la nuée tressaille sur ses franges.

Où est ton sacre? où sont tes anges?
découvre le buisson en feu
sous les couches du temps passé.

Montre-moi pour ce siècle un signe
qui l'empêche de tout traduire
dans un langage dévalué!

Tu me pousses dans l'ombre intime . . .
je pourrais mieux parler sans toi!
donne-moi de dire avec toi.

Bénédiction du Seigneur comme nuit!
bénédiction du Seigneur comme ciel!
terre en marche à son ciel de nuit.

La nuée s'abaisse, elle m'étouffe,
elle me prend et je l'aspire,
elle m'occupe et je la souffle.

PSALM 45

Not only my words, it's me you expect,
me, your word, that I am giving back to you:
before speaking, I was said.

Flood my valleys with your shadow
as you did my heights:
a thick cloud shudders up above.

Where is your crown? where are your angels?
from under layers of the past
you'll unveil a burning bush.

Show me a sign for this century
that will stop us from translating everything
into a baser language!

You push me further into intimate shadow . . .
I could speak better without you!
but give me a way to speak with you.

Night as a blessing of the Lord!
Sky as a blessing of the Lord!
the earth on its way home to night sky.

The cloud comes down, surrounds me,
it takes me and I breathe it in,
it fills me and I breathe it out.

Bénédiction du Seigneur comme vie!
mes paupières se ferment, se rouvrent,
la nuée remue, elle faiblit . . .

Et brusquement c'est la mer Rouge,
toute béante sous mes yeux,
depuis si longtemps derrière eux.

Life as a blessing of the Lord!
my eyelids close, re-open,
the cloud flickers, it fades . . .

And then suddenly the Red Sea
gapes wide before my eyes
after having been for so long behind them.

PSAUME 52

(à celui qui m'attend au sortir du désert,
et narquois, m'interroge sur la manne:)
sans elle, serais-je ici, à livre ouvert?

Rappelle-toi que je menais ma quête
pour lui, pour moi, pour Dieu aussi . . . rappelle-toi:
peut-on ne pas chercher la joie?

Mais tout s'embrouillait dans ma tête . . .
la mort suspendue sur la tête,
qui peut vraiment courir la joie?

Toute voie mène à l'agonie, bien sûr!
il est évident, le futur!
tous les rêves s'y brisent peu à peu.

Alors où devais-je partir?
tu m'as montré ton seuil de l'avenir,
peut-être imprudemment, mon Dieu!

C'est toi qui m'as mené par avance au désert:
par avance? Bien sûr, ce n'était pas encore
l'heure où se déferait ma chair.

Par avance? mais seul, tu peux la devancer!
bien sûr, je ne comprenais rien, je me battais
contre ton vent qui me soufflait:

PSALM 52

(to the one who waits for me at the desert's exit,
and mocking, interrogates me about manna:)
without it, would I be here, with my open book?

Remember that I undertook my quest
for him, for me, also for God . . . remember:
can't one search for joy?

But everything gets muddled in my head . . .
with death hanging over us,
who can really run after joy?

Every way leads to agony, of course.
The future is clear:
little by little all dreams are broken.

So where should I have gone?
you showed me the doorway to your future,
my God, perhaps imprudently.

It's you who led me forward into the desert:
Forward? Of course it wasn't yet
time for my flesh to surrender.

Still forward? but only you can anticipate what's next!
Of course I understood nothing, I fought
against your wind that blew me:

"Viens, c'est toujours un temps de croisade sur terre,
non pas aux lieux de l'infidèle d'autrefois,
mais au sceau de la mort que l'homme porte en soi.

"Viens: ne recherche plus ma tombe dans le monde."
ah! que de temps faut-il pour se voir comme tombe,
que l'âge de l'Église est lent à la briser!

Vaille que vaille, j'ai vécu cet exode,
peut-être imprudemment, je l'ai décrit . . .
quoi? j'avais donc gardé mon livre? le voici.

"Come, it's still the time of the crusades,
not to the places of unbelievers from another time,
but to the seal of death man carries inside himself.

"Come: stop looking for my tomb on earth."
ah! it took so much time to be seen as a tomb
that now the Church is slow to break it.

Worth it or not, I lived through this exodus,
perhaps imprudently, I even described it . . .
What? Did I keep my book? Here it is.

PSAUME 56

(à celui qui m'attend au retour,
porteur du mot "amour" et m'arrête au passage:
ouvre-moi, dit-il, tes bagages)

Toute ma soif de n'avoir rien qui nous sépare
ne me ferait pas sourdre un vrai cri d'amoureux:
seul l'espoir insensé de le crier plus tard . . .

Peut-être sommes-nous des angoisses contraires,
des vies qui pour tenir se font mal ou se nient,
étrangers à n'avoir pas un joint de langage?

Je te dirai pourtant, de mon ombre à ton ombre,
parce que tout l'amour n'est pas levé dans l'ombre:
soyons amis dans la soumission à hiver.

Sans pouvoir découvrir encor ce que recèlent
ces mots d'ami, d'hiver, lancés pour toi vers Dieu,
ce mot de Dieu, comme ténèbre des ténèbres.

Non pas à sens perdu, car voici leur retour,
leur éclosion à la surface du silence:
être quand même en Dieu à si grande distance!

Je suis le voyageur qui n'a pas voulu lire
les mots abstraits des bornes pour se diriger,
et ne peut pas montrer qui a su le conduire.

PSALM 56

(to the one waiting for my return,
carrier of the word "love" who stops me in passing:
open your luggage for me, he says)

All my desire to have nothing separate us
couldn't make a true lover's cry rise out of me:
only a senseless hope to cry it out later on . . .

Perhaps we are contrary torments,
lives who, to hold on, either hurt or deny themselves,
strangers for not having a common language?

But I will say to you, from my shadow to your shadow,
because not all love rises in shadow:
let's be friends in the submission of winter.

Without being able yet to discover what's concealed
in these words of a friend, in winter, hurled for you toward God,
this word of God, like the darkness of all darknesses.

Not because their meaning is lost, for here it returns,
their sense hatching open from silence:
still to be God's from such a great distance!

I am the traveler who didn't want to read
the abstract words on milestones to be directed
and cannot point to who knew which way to go.

Je ne sais que le nom de mon pèlerinage,
celui du pèlerin que j'ai pour passager,
mais ne sois pas déçu si c'est tout mon bagage!

I only know the name of my journey,
that of the pilgrim I am in this passage:
don't be disappointed that's all I carry.

PSAUME 58

Comme un marin s'écrie: la terre!
voici la terre! moi, je clame:
enfin voici l'homme, les hommes!

Jadis je butais dans leurs vignes,
je me heurtais à leurs enceintes
et contre leurs ombres portées.

Mais je n'ai pas fui vers le large:
au contraire, je suis rentré
très loin dans l'homme que j'étais.

Le Seigneur a brûlé mes vignes,
miné de partout mes hauteurs,
il a pris mon ombre à pitié.

Il m'a refait une campagne,
il m'a recouvert de plantiers,
il m'a reformé des collines!

Il me ramène au corps des hommes:
à travers eux, j'entends la fête
des Tabernacles s'annoncer.

La vigne est en fleurs, notre vigne
toute clôture est inutile:
le Seigneur revient vendanger!

PSALM 58

Like a sailor who cries out: Land!
There's land! I shout:
Man! finally I've reached mankind!

Long ago I stumbled through their vineyards,
I dashed toward their pregnant ones
and away from their heavy shadows.

But when I fled I didn't go abroad:
on the contrary, I returned
far into the man I was.

The Lord burned my vines,
cut down what grew tall in me,
he took pity on my shadow.

He remade me as countryside,
he covered me anew with plants,
he reshaped me into hills!

Now he leads me back to mankind:
with them, I gather for
the Feast of Tabernacles.

Now the vine is in bloom, our vine,
and any fence around the vineyard is useless
when the Lord comes back to harvest!

PSAUME 82

Me voici: donne-moi de quoi vivre!
dans un tel noir, que peut-il pousser de bon?

Que de très peu ta voix précède ta lumière!
toi seul qui es bon pousses là.

Pas d'air à respirer sinon ton souffle:
même les plus beaux sens ne te découvrent pas.

Les yeux fermés, comment trouver ma subsistance?
ouverts? toi seul peux les ouvrir à toi.

Prête-moi de ton regard si je dois voir quelque chose,
passe derrière le mien, je verrai ce qu'il faut.

Témoigne pour ton corps, Jésus,
donne-moi ma part de témoin.

Car je frôle mon inconsistance,
je touche l'inanité de tous mes mots.

Je me serai suspect, quoi que je dise;
seul avec toi? je dis seulement: tu es là.

Suis-je sûr d'y être moi-même?
non, c'est plutôt la vie qui passe à travers moi.

A deux! le plus intime, le plus libre!
l'appel et la réponse ne font qu'un.

PSALM 82

Here I am: give me what I need to live!
how could anything good grow in such darkness?

How little your voice precedes your light!
you are the only good that grows there.

No air to breathe if not your breath:
not even the most exquisite senses could find you.

How am I to find my subsistence with closed eyes?
And open? only you can do that.

Lend me your sight if there is something I should see,
with yours behind mine, I will see what is necessary.

And witnessing for your body, Jesus,
assign me my part.

For I brush up against my inadequacy,
I feel the uselessness of my words.

I will suspect myself, whatever I say;
and alone with you? I will only say *there you are*.

Am I even sure of being there myself?
no, it's more life that passes through me.

The two of us! most intimate, most free—
the call and response are the same.

A deux! le même cœur, le plus secret du cœur!
à deux! la gorge et la voix pour le dire!

Two of us! the heart and its secret.
Two of us: the throat and the voice to say so.

PSAUME 88

Dans le secret où tu prépares toute chose,
hâte tes signes à mon coeur.

Trop nombreuses les voix criant ton crépuscule
et tournant contre toi l'affaire du menteur!

Les habitants de ton île s'inquiètent:
n'alourdis pas ta nuit, car ils en ont leur plein.

A quoi ressemblons-nous en te disant lumière,
si nos voix n'en propagent rien?

Prends tes détracteurs à revers,
surprends-les par un coup de main.

Qu'ils crient: C'était vraiment une affaire vitale,
ce que nous avons rejeté!

Nous la pensions tranchée par votre intelligence
et la voici qui reparaît!

Mais toi, tu coupes ma prière:
"Si tu es de mon corps, fais donc mes coups de main!

Te faut-il des visions pour être de mon signe,
des voix pour obéir à mes desseins?"

J'irai donc sur la mer qui menace ton île,
et je te rendrai grâce où tu t'arrêteras.

Que ton serviteur inutile
au moins serve à cela.

PSALM 88

In hiding where you prepare each thing,
hurry your signals to my heart.

Too many are the voices calling you a liar,
clamoring against you in this twilight!

Your island's inhabitants grow anxious:
don't make your night darker when they have had their fill.

How do you think we look, speaking of your radiance
while our voices illuminate nothing?

Come up from behind and catch your detractors off guard,
surprise them with the grip of your hand

so they will cry: "We rejected what was true!
We thought we'd been removed from your brilliance."

But here's where you interrupt my prayer:
"You are of my body, *you* should be the grip of my hand!

Why do you require visions to represent me,
voices to follow my designs?"

Fine: I will go to the sea that threatens your island,
and I will praise you beyond your shore.

So that your unnecessary servant
might at least be useful for that.

PSAUME 90

Tourné vers toi, je t'expose ma charge:
par ta lumière, allège-la!

Puisque mon temps n'est pas achevé à son terme,
mon histoire à son dénouement,

Puisqu'à toute vie pour sa mort,
tu découvres ton avenir,

A mesure que je le dépense,
ton héritage peut grandir.

Oui, je le crois, mais aide ma parole,
serre-la sur la tienne pour la protéger.

Car sans toi ma défaite est irrévocable,
je me détacherais, la désertion me tentera.

Lorsque je fus noué dans le sein de ma mère,
ne me formais-tu pas pour l'alliance avec toi?

Et quand d'autres nœuds se dénouèrent,
ne m'as-tu pas greffé sur celui de la vie?

Tu n'es pas Dieu à bloquer ses approches,
mais qui veut te prendre est saisi.

Et que puis-je ajouter à ton nom de Seigneur?
des mots, des inflexions, tout l'inutile de ma voix.

PSALM 90

Turned toward you I expose my burden:
make it less heavy with your light!

Since my time has not reached its end,
my story its closure,

Since in every life's heading for death
you discover your future,

To the extent that I spend it,
your heritage can grow.

Yes, I believe it, but help my word,
bind it to yours to protect it.

For without you my defeat is irrevocable,
I'll come untied, be tempted by desertion.

When I was fastened to the breast of my mother,
were you not preparing me for an alliance with you?

And when other knots unfastened,
did you not graft me onto life?

You are not a God to block one's approaches,
but one who wants to grasp you is himself seized.

And what can I add to your name of Lord?
words, inflections, all the uselessness of my voice.

Mon Dieu, tu n'es pas un Dieu triste,
ta nuit brûle de joie.

My God, you are not a sad God,
your night burns with joy.

ABOUT THE TRANSLATOR

JENNIFER GROTZ is the author of two books of poetry, *The Needle* and *Cusp*. Her poems, translations, and reviews appear widely in journals such as *The New England Review, Kenyon Review, Ploughshares,* and *The American Poetry Review* as well as in the *Best American Poetry* and *Pushcart Prize* anthologies. She teaches poetry and translation at the University of Rochester and also serves as the Assistant Director of the Bread Loaf Writers' Conference.